A FAMILY LIKE OURS

written by Brooke Culler
illustrated by Agustina Barriola

A story for all to share from generation to generation.

B.C.

No part of this publication may be reproduced in whole or in part, stored in a retrieval system, or transmitted in any form or by any means, electronic, mechanical, photocopying, recording, or otherwise, without prior written permission of the publisher. For information regarding permission, write to the publisher, Storybook Genius, at: 219 Jackson Street, Augusta, Missouri 63332 or visit them at www.sbgpublishing.com. ISBN 978-1-952954-51-1 Text copyright© 2021 Brooke Culler. Illustrations copyright© 2021 Brooke Culler. All rights reserved. Published by Storybook Genius, LLC.

A family like ours is special and sweet,
with love that grows for all we meet.

We always do our chores together,
so that we can help each other.

When the work is through, we laugh and play.
We learn from each other day after day.

...until it's time for teeth and showers.

As we grow older, it's off to school.

We study hard and follow the rules.

We try our best to make you proud
and stand apart from the crowd.

When speed bumps happen, and we need to pout...

...we come together to work it out.

You raise us to be kind and good.

Our lives move on as they should.

We find new jobs and pets and homes.

You remind us that we're never alone.

You grow, too, so we help with chores
like cooking, cleaning, and going to stores.

No matter how young or old we seem,
our family is one unstoppable team!

A family like ours is special and sweet...

....with love that grows for all we meet.

CPSIA information can be obtained
at www.ICGtesting.com
Printed in the USA
BVHW050745111121
621189BV00004B/313